A Little Book of Women's Prayer

A Little Book of Women's Prayer

Compiled by Rachel Stowe

Marshall Pickering
An Imprint of HarperCollins*Publishers*

Marshall Pickering is an Imprint of
HarperCollins*Religious*
Part of HarperCollins*Publishers*
77-85 Fulham Palace Road, London W6 8JB

First published in Great Britain
in 1996 by Marshall Pickering

3 5 7 9 10 8 6 4 2

A catalogue record for this book is available from the British Library

ISBN 0 551 3015 1

Scripture quotations are taken from the New International Version, and also from the
New Revised Standard Version Bible, copyright © 1989 by the Division of Christian Education
of the National Council of the Churches of Christ in the USA.
Used by permission.
All rights reserved.

Printed and bound in Great Britain by
Woolnough Bookbinding Limited, Irthlingborough, Northamptonshire

CONDITIONS OF SALE

Contents

General Acknowledgements

I am most grateful to all those who have contributed to this little book; women of all ages who have written prayers and poems which reflect the great diversity of their situations and locations. Once again, it has been hard to make a choice for there were many more I would have liked to have included had space permitted.

I would particularly like to thank the Mothers' Union diocesan Presidents and Prayer & Spirituality Unit Co-ordinators throughout England, Ireland, Scotland and Wales who responded so willingly to the request for prayers, and to the staff at the MU headquarters at Mary Sumner House, London, for their co-operation and help.

Introduction

'Never a dull moment,' we say as we rush around trying to do half a dozen things at once. More and more women these days are engaged in a juggling act of competing demands from home and family, paid employment, friends and neighbours, voluntary work, social activities. So all too often there is little time to think about their own needs, which then get squeezed to the bottom of a whole pile of other priorities.

This can apply to the spiritual side of life as well. There may well be brief moments of awareness of God at points in a busy day: a smile from a child, a ray of sunshine on a flower, an unexpected kindness from a friend, an encouraging word from a colleague. Momentarily, our hearts rise in thankfulness, but with little time for anything more. And then, maybe we feel guilty, and too easily fall into a downward spiral of not even trying to pray. Our inner life shrivels so that even in the most happy and fulfilled life we wonder just what it is that is missing.

More and more women have other stresses to face. The wearying anxiety of trying to come to terms with redundancy, unemployment, long-term illness or other mishap, increasing age and infirmity, can be so overwhelming that even the mere thought of regular prayer can seem like yet another demand or pressure. For some, the strain of constant care for those unable to care for themselves — the young, the elderly and infirm, the mentally ill and handicapped — can mean there is little personal space in which to pray.

So finally, when we do find ourselves with time to reflect about that spiritual side of life which is such a vital part of us, we may have lost the simple knack of getting in touch with God, of praying.

Prayer is conversation with God; talking to him, listening to him. Even the longest prayer in this little book takes only a minute or so to say, most take only a few seconds, as do the brief passages from the Bible. Tack on a few more seconds of silence and in this short two-way conversation you have maintained your communication with God.

God is always there, ready to listen and talk to us, at any time of day or night. The answer to our requests may be a 'no' or 'not yet' instead of the 'yes' we hope for, because only God can see the full scenario of life. But he understands the pressures we are under, the fears which assail us, the demands which lead us to neglect him, our hesitancy and our stumbling approaches. God encourages us as we try to reflect his love and compassion in our caring for others. He knows our need for peace, for understanding, for forgiveness. He knows and loves each one of us.

Jesus told his followers about the parable of the prodigal son to show us that the loving Father is always waiting for us with outstretched arms, ready to rejoice when we turn to him. This little book has one aim, to help us all in our own turning and returning.

Rachel Stowe

Lord, you are with me

Lord, you are with me as each new day dawns.
> Give me your peace.

Lord, you are with me as I meet others.
> Give me your loving ways.

Lord, you are with me as I go about my work.
> Give me your understanding.

Lord, you are with me as I use my time.
> Give me your compassion.

Lord, you are with me as I end my day.
> Give me your forgiveness.

The Mothers' Union, Carlisle diocese, England

As Each New Day Dawns

❧ Lord, you are with me as each new day dawns.
Give me your peace.

Dear Lord, thank you for yesterday. We give you today, and though we do not know what tomorrow may bring, may we not stray beyond your care and keeping.

Rosemary St John, Alverstoke, Hampshire

In the morning, O Lord, you hear my voice; in the morning I lay my requests before you and wait in expectation. *Psalm 5:3*

Lord, help me to remember that nothing is going to happen to me today that you and I together cannot handle.

Joan Sharples, Mellor St Mary MU, Blackburn, Lancashire

We are hard pressed on every side, but not crushed.

2 Corinthians 4:8

Lord Jesus, we pray that you will help us to see each day not as a toil, but as a blessing.

Julie Bannister, St John the Divine MU, Sandylands, Morecambe, Lancashire

This is the day the Lord has made; let us rejoice and be glad in it. *Psalm 118:24*

Lord, as we begin another day, please guard and guide us on our way. Help us to serve as best we can our families, friends and fellow human beings, to show our faith by love and prayer for others. Grant O Lord that we may be always faithful and true to you.

Susanna Wright, Eccleston St Mary's MU, Chorley, Lancashire

Jesus answered: '"Love the Lord your God with all your heart and with all your soul and with all your strength and with all your mind"; and, "Love your neighbour as yourself."' *Luke 10:27*

Lord, in this quiet time before I start my work, let me be still — and know the light of Christ within. Fill me with your Spirit Lord, give me an inner radiance and peace, so that all whom I meet this day may be blessed by the contact.

Noreen Paveley, Offwell MU, Honiton, Devon

Let the peace of Christ rule in your hearts.

Colossians 3:15

❧

Dear Father, we thank you for bringing us safely to a new day. May your Holy Spirit be with us in thought, word and deed, and guide us to do your will at all times.

St Cuthbert's MU, Bedlington, Northumberland

I will ask the Father, and he will give you another Counsellor to be with you for ever — the Spirit of truth. *John 14:16—17*

5

Dear Father, I awake each new dawn and wonder
what is in store for me. I pray that you will travel
along the road with me each day, whether it be
rough or smooth. Lord, I put my life into
your hands.

Violet Reynolds, Shefford MU, Bedfordshire

But small is the gate and narrow the road that leads
to life. *Matthew 7:14*

All this day, O Lord, let me touch as many
lives as possible for you; and every life I touch, do
you by your Spirit quicken, whether through the
word I speak, the prayer I breathe, or the life I live.

Mary Sumner, Founder of the Mothers' Union (1876)

The path of the righteous is like the first gleam of
dawn, shining ever brighter till the full light of day.

Proverbs 4:18

Lord, you made a perfect world but we are spoiling it. Open our hearts this day that we may learn how to care for your world so that all may live with justice and peace.

Margaret Donald, St Stephen's with St Aidan's, Acomb, York

The earth is the Lord's, and everything in it. *Psalm 24:1*

My Lord and Friend, please help me through this day whatever it may bring. It is lovely having that feeling that you are by my side all the time; you help me in so many ways. Thank you for blessing and caring for me.

Iris Stubbington, Eastleigh MU, Hampshire

Let not your heart be troubled, neither let it be afraid. *John 14:27*

Lord Jesus, give me the faith to reach out to you with every need, trusting in your great love and concern for each one of us. And give me the faith to expect my life to be changed.

Revd Jacqueline Henry, Tiptree, Essex

We will all be changed — in a flash, in the twinkling of an eye, at the last trumpet. *1 Corinthians 15.51–52*

❧

Dear Father in heaven, may Jesus bring comfort and strength to those who face each day knowing that their time on earth is limited. Teach us all to treasure each day and to look for quality rather than quantity of life. May we take time to observe the beauty around us and to thank you each day for sharing it with us.

Pamela Mullan, Derryloran MU, Cookstown, County Tyrone

God has said, 'Never will I leave you; never will I forsake you.' *Hebrews 13:5*

Hold my hand, Lord, as I enter each new day – may every step along the way be with you beside me; may every word I speak be spoken in accordance with your love; may my every action be guided by my awareness of your presence, so that as I come to evening I may lie down with peace in my heart, knowing that you are there.

Anthea Toft, Cardington MU, Church Stretton, Shropshire

So we say with confidence, 'The Lord is my helper; I will not be afraid.' *Hebrews 13:6*

Lord Jesus Christ, be with me through this day; give me your peace of mind and teach me to be loving and kind. Give love and help to those in

need and keep my family safe and sound from
all evil. May greed, hate and violence cease and
let the whole world know your peace.

Doris Everitt, All Saints' MU, St Mary's Bay, Kent

Live in peace with each other. *1 Thessalonians 5:13*

Dear Lord and Saviour, we thank you for taking
care of us through the night. May we know and
feel your presence with us as we go about our daily
work and know that you are helping and guiding
us in all that we do.

*Eveline Sellers, St John the Divine MU, Sandylands, Morecambe,
Lancashire*

He guides the humble in what is right and teaches
them his way. *Psalm 25:9*

Heavenly Father, thank you for this new day.
Thank you for the fulfilment of your promise and
commitment in the sunrise. Forgive me my sins,
show me your will for today and give me your
strength to do it.

You give me your love in abundance; please give
me the grace to share it with those whom you will
give me to meet today.

Joan Wilkins, Emmanuel MU, Northwood, London

Every promise has been fulfilled; not one has failed.

Joshua 23:14

Lord Jesus, help me through each day in all I
think and do and say. Help me to be good and
kind so your love shines through and maybe
eases a troubled mind through a word or a smile.

Bless me as I witness for you, and give me
strength and courage as I journey on my way.

Muriel Quinton, St John's MU, Redhill, Surrey

Because of the Lord's great love we are not
consumed, for his compassions never fail. They
are new every morning; great is your faithfulness.

Lamentations 3:22—23

Dear Lord, we thank you for the dawning of
each new day, bringing with it opportunities to serve
you anew. Help us not to waste those opportunities
but to take delight in your service hour by hour,
remembering that you were the servant of all.
Strengthen our faith and that of our loved ones each
day by the power of your Holy Spirit, and when it is
time to lie down and rest, may we be aware of your
comforting presence.

Dorothy Robinson, Ecclesfield, South Yorkshire

Where morning dawns and evening fades you call
forth songs of joy. *Psalm 65:8*

O Lord my God, as once again I open my eyes to
the dawn of a new day, I thank you for the gift of
sight to behold the wonderful things you have
created all around us. I thank you for the gift of
smell to appreciate the scent of the flowers in the
gardens, fields and hedgerows, and for being able
to touch and taste the fruit and vegetables you
have provided for us.

I ask you to protect me from all the evils of this
day and to guide me to do and say always what is
right in your sight.

Edith Elliot, Moy & Charlemont MU, *County Tyrone*

O Lord, our Sovereign, how majestic is your name
in all the earth! *Psalm 8:1*

Lord, fill me with your love that I may use it
  to love others.
Lord, fill me with your love that I may have
  no room for sin.
Lord, fill me with your love that I may be able
  to forgive.
Lord, fill me with your love that I may have
  humility.
Lord, fill me with your love that I may love
  you Lord, every moment of the day.

Dorothy Dowling, Newbiggin MU, Newcastle

Dear friends, let us love one another, for love comes
from God. *1 John 4:7*

❧

In the dawn of life re-awakening: Lord speak to me.
In the middle of life's daily chores: Lord speak to me.
At the start of daily struggles: Lord speak to me.

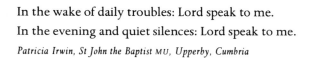

In the wake of daily troubles: Lord speak to me.
In the evening and quiet silences: Lord speak to me.

Patricia Irwin, St John the Baptist MU, *Upperby, Cumbria*

The Lord is my shepherd, I shall not be in want. He makes me lie down in green pastures, he leads me beside quiet waters, he restores my soul. *Psalm 23:1–3*

Dear Father, may your presence be with me this
  day as I rise to comfort the baby and watch the
  departures for work and school.
Dear Father, may your presence be with me this
  day, as I clean the house and prepare the food.
Dear Father, may your presence be with me this
  day in the supermarket and at the school gate.
Dear Father, may your presence be with me this
  day as I dry the dishes and bandage a knee.

Dear Father, may your presence be in my home, in my deeds and in my heart, this day and every day.

Sylvia Leonard, MU Action & Outreach Representative, Newcastle diocese

She watches over the affairs of the household and does not eat the bread of idleness. *Proverbs 31:27*

∾

Dear Lord, help me to dedicate this day and all my days to your glory. Without your help I cannot forget myself. Please help me to listen to other people's problems and not overwhelm them with mine; to seek out the lonely and be a friend, to smile at people I pass on the way. Help me to work quietly and efficiently and not for self-gratification (does it really matter if no one praises me for a job well done when in my heart I do it only for you?).

I know that at times I will fail, but the knowledge

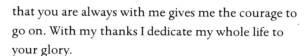

that you are always with me gives me the courage to go on. With my thanks I dedicate my whole life to your glory.

Heather Le Galley, MU Prayer & Spirituality Co-ordinator, Guernsey

Your Father, who sees what is done in secret, will reward you. *Matthew 6:4*

Good morning, God, you are ushering in
    another day untouched and freshly new,
So here I come to ask you, God, if you will
    renew me too.
Forgive the many errors that I made yesterday
And let me try again dear God to walk closer
    in your way.
But, Father, I am well aware I cannot make it
    on my own

So take my hand and hold it tight, for I
  cannot walk alone.

Wilma Ross, St John's MU, Dumfries, Dumfries & Galloway

O Lord, listen! O Lord, forgive! *Daniel 9:19*

Jesus love me, take my hands,
  Teach me to obey your commands.
  Each morning wake me with a prayer,
  Let me know that you are there.

Through the day and through the night,
  Jesus, be my guiding light.
  When my life on earth is through,
  Jesus, let me dwell in you.

Elizabeth Webster, St Cyprian's Church, Owlthorpe, Sheffield

For God who said 'Let light shine out of darkness,' made his light shine in our hearts to give us the light of the knowledge of the glory of God in the face of Christ. *2 Corinthians 4:6*

As I Meet Others

❧ Lord, you are with me as I meet others.
   Give me your loving ways.

Lord Jesus — my face is like a mirror — if I smile,
so will others. Help me to mirror you so that the
people I meet will see a little of you in me.

Diana Jones, Llyswen, Brecon, Powys

And we, who with unveiled faces all reflect the
Lord's glory, are being transformed into his likeness
with ever-increasing glory, which comes from the
Lord, who is the Spirit. *2 Corinthians 3:18*

O Lord, help us to be construction workers in the
world of broken relationships. Let us work on bridges,
not barricades, highways and not road blocks.

Lothingland Deanery MU, Norwich diocese

Carry each other's burdens, and in this way you will
fulfil the law of Christ. *Galatians 6:2*

Heavenly Father, whose Son Jesus Christ went about healing the sick, guide us in word and action to cheer and comfort. As you have compassion so give us your compassion and your gifts of peace and healing.

St Peter's MU, Pertenhall, Bedfordshire

... and ... to another gifts of healing by the one Spirit. *1 Corinthians 12:8–9*

O Lord, bless those who care for others. Strengthen them for the work their hands have to do. In the early hours, when your presence is most near, pour down on them the courage, fortitude and humour needed to continue their labour of love.

Margaret Mitchell, Christ Church MU, Liversedge, West Yorkshire

Dear children, let us not love with words or tongue but with actions and in truth. *1 John 3:18*

Lord, be with us, that all with whom we speak may hear you; Lord be with us, that all with whom we meet may see your love and compassion; Lord be with us, that all hearts may be set on fire for you and be uplifted to you in praise and glory, this day.

Rachel Nugee, Central President of the MU, 1977–82

He will baptize you with the Holy Spirit and with fire. *Luke 3:16*

Heavenly Father, thank you for the world. Give us the spirit of faith and hope to do your will. We pray for peace and unity among all nations; freedom for hostages, shelter for the homeless, food for the hungry, medication for the sick. Lord Jesus, hear our prayer.

Betty Robertson, St John the Baptist MU, Stockton-on-Tees, Cleveland

Sing to the Lord, all the earth; proclaim his salvation day after day. *1 Chronicles 16:23*

We remember Lord those who have never had a word of kindness spoken to them. Give us that love which is patient and kind, that we may reach some cold heart today and warm it with some simple act of kindness.

Lady Jean Coggan, Winchester

Anxiety weighs down the human heart, but a good word cheers it up. *Proverbs 12:25*

Dear Lord and Father, we thank you for the beauty of your creation; for the hills and vales, trees and flowers, the majesty of mountains; the seasons, each with their own particular beauty.

May we always be aware that we are part of that creation and respect it.

Cath Eales, Bath Abbey MU, Bath, Avon

You care for the land and water it; you enrich it abundantly. *Psalm 65:9*

Dear Lord, we thank you for the beauty and sounds in the world. We ask your blessing on all people who cannot see or hear their loved ones, or the sight and sounds of animals and birds, or the sound of music, which we take for granted. Lord in your mercy: hear our prayer.

Stockton Parish Church MU, Stockton-on-Tees, Cleveland

We live by faith, not by sight. *2 Corinthians 5:7*

O Lord our God, wherever you are allowed to
be King there is peace and justice. We pray for all
those whose desire is to live at peace with their
neighbours. Empower them to be peacemakers by
arming them with your compassion. We pray for all
who seek to perpetrate hatred and violence: disarm
them by melting their hearts with your love.

Val Brookes, MU Prayer Correspondent, diocese of Dublin & Glendalough

The fruit of righteousness will be peace. *Isaiah 32:17*

Dear Father, bestow upon us the ability to listen.
Through the power of prayer Lord help us to hear
and fully understand the truth of your word,
enabling us to live a life worthy of your calling.
Keep us always alert and attentive, heeding every
opportunity to enrich the lives and well-being of
others.

The Mothers' Union, Llandaff diocese

Fools think their own way is right, but the wise listen to advice. *Proverbs 12:15*

Dear Lord, we pray for those whose lives are affected by alcohol dependency. We ask that you will show them new ways to cope with the problems which lead them to drink. We pray too for all families disrupted by alcohol abuse that they may know your love.

Withington Deanery MU, Manchester

Do not get drunk on wine, which leads to debauchery. Instead, be filled with the spirit.
Ephesians 5:18

Dear Lord, life, it seems, is like a sea, with calm or stormy weather. Please help us to keep our families safe and with your help ride out the storms together. When life is good and seas are calm, help us to pray for those in stormy waters that they will find as we have done, safe anchorage in your love.

Margaret Jones, St Matthias, Treharris, Mid Glamorgan

He stilled the storm to a whisper; the waves of the sea were hushed. *Psalm 107:29*

O God our heavenly Father, we thank you for our parish church with its friendliness and love, and for the staff who care for its welfare and worship. Bless all who enter your churches throughout the world; give us joy and patience with each other and enrich our lives with your love.

Edith Kennon, St John the Baptist MU, Upperby, Cumbria

Now to him who is able to do immeasurably more than all we ask or imagine, according to his power that is at work within us, to him be glory in the church and in Christ Jesus throughout all generations. *Ephesians 3:20—21*

Father, forgive me for looking the other way, for thinking that the things I have to do are more important than people. Forgive me for the many times I have not really listened, for the careless word spoken or the help not given; for the vain thoughts and hurtful silences, for any hurt I have inflicted unknowingly. Teach me to cross out the 'I' and to seek only to follow you in word and action.

Kitty Cooper, MU Prayer & Spirituality Co-ordinator, Wakefield diocese

A priest happened to be going down the same road, and when he saw the man, he passed by on the other side. *Luke 10:31*

Loving heavenly Father, your Son endured the loneliness of the desert and his parents moved to a strange land; we ask that you bless and sustain those undergoing the upheaval of moving house. May they find a loving welcome in their new home and know that you are always near.

The Mothers' Union, Province of Ireland

The Lord said to Abram 'Leave your country, your people and your father's household and go to the land I will show you.' *Genesis 12:1*

Heavenly Father, you know the stresses and strains of modern life. We ask your blessing on those

making a home together. May they have joy
in their loving, tolerance and understanding in
times of disagreement, security in the rush of
daily living, and may they come to know the
richness of your love.

Beryl Denney, St Mary's MU, Theydon Bois, Essex

Be kind and compassionate to one another,
forgiving each other, just as in Christ God forgave
you. *Ephesians 4:32*

❧

Heavenly Father, we thank you for the blessing of
family life and pray for all parents, godparents,
junior church leaders, schoolteachers, and all who
are concerned with bringing up children. We
remember those children whom society has failed,
who have been abused or deprived of moral
teaching. We pray for them, and for social workers,
special needs teachers, probation officers, chaplains

and all who are working to restore them to health
of body and mind.

St Andrew's Church, Sharrow, Sheffield

Let the little children come to me, and do not
hinder them, for the Kingdom of God belongs to
such as these. *Mark 10:14*

Dear heavenly Father, whose love is world-wide,
may we who have so many blessings never take
them for granted, and never forget those of your
children in other parts of the world who suffer
grievious want and deprivation. We commend all
who suffer in any way to your tender care. May we
in our small way never miss an opportunity to
help wherever we can.

Margaret Oakley, Christ Church, Fulwood, Sheffield

Is there anyone among you who, if your child asks
for bread, will give a stone? *Matthew 7:9*

Almighty God, who made of one blood all nations
who dwell in the world, bless this world and bring
quickly the day when colour and race shall no
longer divide us. Give your help in those places
where new nations are born; grant that bitterness
and hatred will not destroy fellowship and peace,
and hasten the time when the knowledge of you
will cover the earth as the waters cover the sea.

Margaret Buckley, St Saviour's MU, Thirlstone, South Yorkshire

For the earth will be filled with the knowledge of
the glory of the Lord, as the waters cover the sea.

Habakkuk 2:14

Heavenly Father, remembering that your Son grew up in an earthly home, we thank you for the joys and responsibilities of parenthood. We pray for all birth mothers, stepmothers, adoptive and foster-mothers, and for all men and women who fulfil the role of parents, whether alone or in partnership, that your grace may be upon them, and your loving strength uphold them in all difficulties.

St Andrew's Church, Sharrow, Sheffield

His mother said to him 'Son, why have you treated us like this? Your father and I have been anxiously searching for you.' *Luke 2:48*

Heavenly Father, be with us in our homes; bless our children, grandchildren, nieces, nephews and godchildren. Help us to set them a good example and never mislead them by our words and actions. When they bring us their secrets help us to listen

with respect and understanding. Sometimes
they seem to be far from us; help us to be wise
and patient, and at all times to trust in you so
they may see in us the difference it makes to live
close to you and experience your love.

Ella Appleton, Rothersthorpe & Kislingbury MU, *Northamptonshire*

I have been reminded of your sincere faith, which
first lived in your grandmother Lois and in your
mother Eunice. *2 Timothy 1:5*

O Lord and heavenly Father, you are the giver
of life, and life is a book we all must read. We thank
you for the life of each and every one of us; for
our families, our loved ones and our friends. You
know all our secrets; help us to trust you with our
future and give us strength to face each new day.

We pray that we may all come to know and love
you as we turn the daily page of our book of life.

Isa Baildon, Penrith, Cumbria

Another book was opened, which is the book of life.

Revelation 20:12

Heavenly Father, we cannot understand why there
is so much misery in our world. This is not how you
meant it to be and we know that it is because of the
evil in us all. Please help us; be with all those who
are crying out for help through neglect, cruelty,
hunger, illness or loneliness.

Give strength and wisdom to all carers, social
workers, voluntary services and all groups and
individuals who do care and who try to help. Let
your love and compassion show in their lives,
and show us how we too can play our part in
love and service.

Pat McDonagh, St John the Baptist's MU, Royston, South Yorkshire

Truly I tell you, just as you did it to one of the least
of these who are members of my family, you did it
to me. *Matthew 25:40*

Lord of all, we give you praise and thanks for all
your goodness to us. We thank you that you have
given different gifts to each of us for the building up
of the church, the Body of Christ. Help us always to
use our gifts wisely, sensitively, generously and
graciously. We thank you for our fellowship within
the church; help us at all times to make others

welcome, to enable each other to grow in faith, to
inspire and encourage each other, so that we may
become channels of your love, peace and
forgiveness.

St John the Baptist MU, Upperby, Cumbria

Now you are the body of Christ, and each one of you
is a part of it. *1 Corinthians 12:27*

As I Go About My Work

∾ Lord, you are with me as I go about my work.
Give me your understanding.

Dear Lord, strengthen me to do my tasks today,
and though some things are hard to do, some
people hard to understand, comfort me as
you always do.

Elsie Mansergh, Ainsdale St John's MU, Southport, Merseyside

May the favour of the Lord our God rest upon us;
establish the work of our hands for us. *Psalm 90:17*

Holy Spirit, I must make a decision in the next few
minutes. Show me plainly what is God's will.

*Joy Hawthorne, MU Prayer & Spirituality Unit Co-ordinator,
Manchester diocese*

Father, if you are willing, remove this cup from me;
yet, not my will but yours be done. *Luke 22:42*

Dear Father, help us to discern the 'Spirit of the Living Christ' in the ordinary mundane happenings of our everyday lives, and to respond and reach out with your love and wisdom as shown us by Jesus.

Bunty Jones, Eardisley Group MU, Herefordshire

The fruit of the Spirit is love, joy, peace, patience, kindness, goodness, faithfulness, gentleness and self-control. *Galatians 5:22–23*

Lord, you are in all the people I meet at work: the young mum, the old lady with a smile on her face, the man with a joke on his lips. You are in me as I talk with people and pray that some of your love shows through in the things I say and in the look on my face.

Anne Rimmer, St John the Baptist, Burscough Bridge, Lancashire

Be imitators of God, therefore, as dearly loved
children and live a life of love, just as Christ loved us
and gave himself up for us. *Ephesians 5:1–2*

Lord, I'm lost! I'm stuck on the road in the darkness.
Shine your light before me to guide my feet; give me
your hand to keep me from stumbling; walk with
me until I find your path again.

Ricky Chilvers, Market Deeping MU, *Peterborough*

When Jesus spoke again to the people, he said, 'I am
the light of the world. Whoever follows me will
never walk in darkness, but will have the light of
life.' *John 8:12*

Lord, I am feeling lost today, uncertain of who I am
and what I am doing in your world. I want so much to
serve you, but I feel useless, confused and bewildered.

Renew my confidence, my trust and my hope, and fill
me with your Holy Spirit, for Jesus' sake.

Joy Hawthorne, MU Prayer & Spirituality Unit Co-ordinator,
Manchester diocese

Praise be to the God and Father of our Lord Jesus
Christ! In his great mercy he has given us new birth
into a living hope through the resurrection of Jesus
Christ from the dead.   *1 Peter 1:3*

❧

Father, give us strength to cope with the fast pace
and the constant changes in our world today. Help
us always to make the right decisions when needed.
Give us compassion in our dealings with all people,
particularly with those whose ways are different
from ours. Give us your guidance in all we think, say
and do; fill us with the power, the love and the joy
of your Spirit.

Pickering Deanery MU, North Yorkshire

46

Do not conform any longer to the pattern of this world, but be transformed by the renewing of your mind. Then you will be able to test and approve what God's will is — his good, pleasing and perfect will. *Romans 12:2*

Lord, we bring to you the thousands who are unemployed, and those facing redundancy with little hope of ever working again. We pray too for young people who have never known employment. Give them courage to face each new day. In your mercy, Lord, show us the way forward, guide our leaders, and help us to have pride in our work and in ourselves.

Iris Jubber, St Bartholomew's MU, Gourock, Renfrewshire

Even the very hairs of your head are numbered. So don't be afraid; you are worth more than many sparrows. *Matthew 10:30–31*

Dear Lord God, please take hold of us and make us see how we are damaging your beautiful world by the nature of our lifestyles. Please forgive our misdeeds and lead us towards reparation, conservation and caring.

Eileen Bethell, Good Shepherd MU, Furnham, Somerset

God saw all that he had made, and it was very good.

Genesis 1:31

Dear Lord, we pray for those who lead, for those who have power, and for those who train and influence others. May they seek your wisdom, your will and your honour in fulfilling their responsibilities, especially in working for peace.

Christ Church, North Finchley, London

If any of you is lacking in wisdom, ask God, who gives to all generously and ungrudgingly, and it will be given you. *James 1:5*

Dear heavenly Father, we bring before you all the nations of your world who are not at peace. We pray that leaders may be influenced by your love and learn to live together without war. We pray for those actively involved in fighting and ask you to comfort their families. We pray for children in war-torn countries; inspire the rest of us around your world to do all we can to rehabilitate these little children.

Maureen Limbrick, Yaxley MU, Ely diocese

Blessed are the peacemakers, for they will be called children of God. *Matthew 5:9*

Keep us faithful in prayer O God; may your Holy
Spirit light the way forward in every aspect of our
parish life and of your ministry through it. May
your truth direct our dealings and your love
enable us to respond in loving obedience to you.
We pray for your blessing and protection upon
all those who work for your kingdom, especially
for our missionaries who work far from home;
may your loving presence be always with them.

Christ Church, North Finchley, London

Go therefore and make disciples of all nations.

Matthew 28:19

∾

Almighty God, who with your Son, Jesus Christ,
realized that the practical duties of life are
necessary, we humbly beseech you that in our
duty of cleaning the church, by your grace and
with your help in we may beautify this place of

worship, that all who enter here may be led to
praise you more sincerely.

St Fin Barre's MU, Cork Cathedral

The Lord has assigned to each his task.

1 Corinthians 3:5

Thank you, Father, for all that our Mothers' Union
membership enables us to do in your service and
for the opportunities it offers. Lead and inspire us
as we try to help young parents in our community,
the elderly, the children and all who you bring to
us each day, that by cheerfully offering a helping
hand and a listening ear your love may be given
and received and your name honoured.

St Gregory's MU, Goodleigh, Devon

In Joppa there was a disciple named Tabitha (which, when translated, is Dorcas), who was always doing good and helping the poor. *Acts 9:36*

Dear Lord, help us, guide us, protect us and give us your strength in all situations; to follow our daily tasks without complaint, to honour your name and praise you for your love. May the work of the Mothers' Union continue to flourish and be one means of spreading your message throughout the world.

Irene Greenall, Withnell, Lancashire

Give us today our daily bread. *Matthew 6:11*

'Come on, we've no time to lose
Please remember to tie your shoes.
Is your homework up to date?

Do hurry up or we'll be late,
For the bus will be at the gate
And you know he will not wait.'
    Dear Lord, help me to keep my cool
    Whilst I get the children off to school.

Martha Gash, St Deny's MU, Sleaford, Lincolnshire

Cast all your anxiety on him, because he cares for you. *1 Peter 5:7*

School holidays again – so nudge me Lord! Give me patience and understanding with the children today. So much needs to be done to feed them all, then there's the washing, cleaning and shopping. Help me to realize that loving them and teaching them about you is much more important than a tidy home. Remind me to bite back the criticism and to praise whenever possible; to ask politely and to thank; to listen intently and answer

carefully. I so often need your reminder — so
nudge me, Lord!

Kathleen Andrews, St Mary's, Brecon, Powys

Love is patient, love is kind.   *1 Corinthians 13:4*

Lord, we pray for the safety of all children,
especially during school holidays. Many will be
left unsupervised, vulnerable, given drugs, led
into violence and crime, ruining their own lives
and the lives of others. Forgive us where our
discipleship has failed; strengthen us and help us.
Let the light of your gospel shine into all the
dark corners of our society so that children
everywhere may have safe and happy homes
and be brought up to live godly lives.

Kay Joures, St Oswin's MU, Wylam, Northumberland

Jesus said to his disciples: 'Things that cause people
to sin are bound to come, but woe to that person
through whom they come.' *Luke 17:1*

O God our Father, guide us and all who have
the care of children with love, patience and
understanding. We pray especially for those in
our Sunday Schools and Parent and Toddler groups;
may we help and encourage them towards
independence and maturity. Strengthen young
parents in the knowledge of your love and
give them your joy and peace.

*Freda English, St Peter & St Paul MU, Weedon Bec,
Northamptonshire*

After three days they found him in the temple
courts, sitting among the teachers, listening to them
and asking them questions. *Luke 2:46*

Father: be with me to give me love,
Son: be near me to give me joy,
Spirit: be in me to give me power.
Love in my heart this day,
Joy in my living this day,
Power in my working this day.
Blessed Three in One be with me, near me,
    and in me.

Mary Liver, Bowston, Cumbria

May the grace of the Lord Jesus Christ, and the love
of God, and the fellowship of the Holy Spirit be with
you all. *2 Corinthians 13:14*

We thank you, Lord, for our families; and
    remember those who are lonely and have no
    loved ones.
We thank you for our homes; and pray for those
    who have no shelter.

We thank you for our work; and pray for those
    who are unemployed.
We thank you for our health; and pray for those
    who are sick in mind or body.
Dear Father, be with us all in our various
    situations.

Rothbury MU, Morpeth, Northumberland

'Sir,' the invalid replied, 'I have no one to help me
into the pool when the water is stirred.' *John 5:7*

❧

Father of all, you showed us in word and deed that
children are precious to you. Thank you for all that
they bring to us; help us to nurture them in
goodness.

    Let us not forget that for every child who grows
up in the knowledge of your love there are many
more who know nothing of your ways; help us to
accept responsibility for them all.

Let us not forget that for every child who laughs, there are many more who weep; help us to reach out to them by showing concern for their needs.

Let us not forget that for every child who is well fed, there are many more who starve; forgive our greed and lack of concern.

Bless all agencies whose work is for the good of children and bless all who care for children; inspire them with truth and enfold them in your love.

Kate Watson, Holy Nativity MU, Newcastle

And he took the children in his arms, put his hands on them and blessed them. *Mark 10:16*

Dear Lord, we thank you for our workaday world; for the milkman and the postman on their rounds; for the doctor and district nurse on theirs; for care assistants, meals-on-wheels and the voluntary services. We thank you for the

busy shops and markets and the huge lorries
taking our food to the supermarkets. We thank
you for the preparation and partaking of each
meal by our families, remembering with sorrow
those who have nothing on their plates. And
finally, Lord, we thank you that after our busy
day we can pass each night in peaceful slumber,
as the rhythm of the day ends and your angels
guard our beds.

Renee Preston, Paganhill MU, Bisley, Gloucestershire

Each of you should look not only to your own
interests, but also to the interests of others.

Philippians 2:4

My Lord and my God; I imagine a snowy
    mountain: I think of your purity and ask
        to be kept from wrongdoing.
I imagine a flower-filled countryside; I think

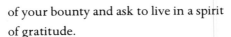

of your bounty and ask to live in a spirit
of gratitude.

I imagine a summer breeze in the pine trees;
I think of your nearness and ask for your
guidance.

I imagine a fetid hospital ward; I think of
you curing the lepers and ask for your
healing power for the sick and your comfort
for the dying.

I imagine an ugly urban housing estate; I think
of you mingling with the crowds and ask that
your concern and pity may be present there.

I imagine a war-torn city; I think of your
condemnation of the swords and staves in
Gethsemane, and ask for your peace and
justice throughout the world.

Frances Mason, St Andrew's Church, Norton, Powys

Jesus went through all the towns and villages,
teaching in their synagogues, preaching the good
news of the kingdom and healing every disease and
sickness. *Matthew 9:35*

❧

Lord, be with me as I drive today,
Guide and guard me all the way,
Through fog and sunshine, wind and rain
Lead me safely home again.

Hazards and dangers I shall meet;
Be in my hands, my eyes, my feet.
Aid my judgement, clear my mind,
So through the maze my route I'll find.

May I forgive the fools who speed
And cut in close when there's no need.
Keep me calm and let no anger
Tempt me into further danger.

When passed by one whose car is new
Let no envy cloud my view.
May patience teach me to discern
Anxiety in those who learn.

Let me act well — yet guard me still
From undue pride in driving skill;
For boastful show-off risks once taken
May prove my 'skilfulness' mistaken.

Lord, in your mercy, hear my prayer:
May I perceive you everywhere,
Till safely through life's twisting bends
I give you thanks at Journey's End.

Edna Eglinton, North Tawton, Devon

I proclaimed a fast, so that we might humble
ourselves before our God and ask him for a safe
journey for us and our children. *Ezra 8:21*

As I Use My Time

❧ Lord, you are with me as I use my time.
   Give me your compassion.

Heavenly Father, thank you for the promise of your Holy Spirit to enable me to speak about you. Help me to create more time to listen and learn from your word; I long to serve you better. Please forgive my shortcomings.

Jane Parkinson, MU Prayer & Spirituality Unit Co-ordinator, Bradford diocese

Men and women moved by the Holy Spirit spoke from God. *2 Peter 1:21*

❧

Be with us Lord in all we do; forgive us Lord for all we fail to do; and help us Lord to be with you through Jesus Christ your Son.

Marion Holmes, St Michael & St Helen's, Almondbury, West Yorkshire

Forgive as the Lord forgave you. *Colossians 3:13*

Lord, I'm running late again! I know, I'm always doing it. Please make me keep an eye on the time.

Joy Hawthorne, MU Prayer & Spirituality Unit Co-ordinator, Manchester diocese

There is a time for everything, and a season for every activity under heaven. *Ecclesiastes 3:1*

Almighty God, who gives us strength to cope with the stresses and details of our daily lives, grant us the power of your Holy Spirit so that we may be able to keep cheerful and calm, showing your love to others.

MU, diocese of Limerick & Killaloe

Since we live by the Spirit, let us keep in step with the Spirit. *Galatians 5:25*

A friend confided her anxieties to me today, Lord.
Help me to keep my mouth shut and my heart and
mind open to your guidance. We both need your
wisdom and love in her situation and we know that,
if we ask, it will be freely given.

Brenda Preece, Much Dewchurch MU, Hereford

I sought the Lord, and he answered me, and
delivered me from all my fears. *Psalm 34:4*

Lord, I do not find you in the noise and bustle of my
busy life but in the quiet moments, so teach me to
pause more often and help me to hear your voice in
the stillness.

Joyce Jenkins, Diocesan Trustee, Swansea & Brecon MU

Listen! I am standing at the door, knocking; if you
hear my voice and open the door, I will come in to
you. *Revelation 3:20*

O God our Father, God of mercy, love and grace;
teach us to be still so that within the inmost centre
of our being we may know your presence. Teach
us to be still that our minds may listen to your
guidance. Teach us to empty our hearts of self so
that you can fill them with yourself and make us
channels through which your healing love will
flow to those for whom we pray.

Eileen Bethell, Good Shepherd MU, Furnham, Somerset

I pray that out of his glorious riches he may
strengthen you with power through his Spirit in
your inner being. *Ephesians 3:16*

Heavenly Father,
Make us more sensitive to the reality of your
    constant presence,
Make me more sensitive to the hearing of your voice,

Make me more sensitive to the understanding of
   your guidance and
Make me more sensitive to the awareness of your
   enveloping love.

Berwick MU, Berwick-upon-Tweed, Northumberland

And that you may love the Lord your God, listen to
his voice, and hold fast to him. *Deuteronomy 30:20*

Father, during our busy daily lives teach us to be
spontaneous in worshipping you. Whenever we are
overwhelmed by the wonders of nature or life itself
let us be still and stand in awe and gratitude and say
'Thank you Lord.'

   Lord, kindle within us a reverence for life and
teach us to cherish the wonders of your universe.

Hazel Fountain, MU Prayer & Spirituality Co-ordinator, Peterborough diocese

Be still, and know that I am God. *Psalm 46:10*

Thank you, God, for sunsets and trees; for roses and soft breezes; for birds and mountains, grass and fountains; for friends and quiet times; for your presence and strength in times of need. We thank you for all these things.

Pamela Mullan, Derryloran MU, Cookstown, County Tyrone

The Lord is the everlasting God, the Creator of the ends of the earth. *Isaiah 40:28*

God of the morning, we pray for strength.
God of noontide, we pray for the hungry.
God of the evening, we pray for fellowship.
God of night-time, grant us peace.

Pickering Deanery MU, North Yorkshire

Do not be anxious about anything, but in everything, by prayer and thanksgiving, present your requests to God. *Philippians 4:6*

Lord, you are kind, your generosity overwhelms us. Thank you for the inner strength given in adversity, for the individual gifts given to us to share. We thank you for people who have patience and listening skills, and for those who have passed their wisdom and experience down from one generation to another.

Patricia Molloy, Bangor diocese

We have different gifts, according to the grace given us. *Romans 12:6*

Dear Father, in our busy lives – guide us; in our sorrows – comfort us; in our joys – give us grateful hearts. May we listen to others and be open to the needs of our neighbours near and far. Be with our families and friends and help us to trust them into your hands; may your Holy Spirit enfold us and keep us now and always.

Marjorie Sims, Dunchurch MU, Rugby, Warwickshire

But they who wait for the Lord shall renew their strength. *Isaiah 40:31*

I come to you, Lord, an expectant mother, for the gift of patience. There are days when I walk on air, and days when I seem to grow tired of waiting. Lord, I feel I must look around me more to notice the rhythm of nature in the gardens, the countryside; to accept the need for sleep and rest, for work and recreation; to accept that it takes nine months for a child to be born; to know that delays are in the nature of things. Teach me that I live in your world and not mine, that you are in charge. I come to you, Lord, for your gift of patience.

Hilda Andrews, 'A Precious Gift: Prayers for mothers-to-be',
Winchester diocese

My soul glorifies the Lord and my spirit rejoices in God my Saviour. *Luke 1:46—47*

Where do I find you? I find you in quietness,
Lord. I look upwards and see the sky; it was there
yesterday, today, and it will be tomorrow. The
sun shines in all its glory and I think of your face
smiling down on me. A gentle breeze rustles the
leaves on the trees as if you are passing by, to see
that all is well in my little world. I hear you in
the laughter and delight of a little child, and see
you in the beauty and innocence of a new-born
babe. Who else could perform such a miracle?
Thank you Lord for giving me the eyes to see and
the ears to hear of your many wonders. I have so
little to offer, but what I do have I share lovingly
and willingly with you and for you. Where do I
find you, Lord? Everywhere.

Sally Roberts, All Saints' Church, Edmonton, London

If I go up to the heavens, you are there; if I make my
bed in the depths, you are there. *Psalm 139:8*

There's the telephone again, Lord, janging my tired
nerves. Please, not another cry for help; I'm so tired
and weary. I have nothing left to give now Lord. I'm
so bad at saying 'no'. Please help me Lord, be with
me as I answer, help me to listen quietly, lovingly,
to say the right thing, to be helpful and honest Lord.

  'Hello ...'

Thank you Father for caring, for lifting me,
refreshing me. I'm walking on air now, Lord, simply
because someone cared about me, someone called
me to show love, to offer help and ease my
workload. Someone noticed. Thank you Lord for
ringing me.

Eunice Norwood, Wembley, London

So in everything, do to others what you would have
them do to you. *Matthew 7:12*

If every moment, every breath and act is prayer —
what of the angry words, the sudden, unexpected
curse, the cruel comment, the bit of gossip we could
not resist, the quick lie to save the moment?

Father, hear even these and do not hide from
them; turn back each unworthy word or deed so we
may know them for what they are and be ashamed.
But, as you hear them, be our doctor too; root out
the cause — turn those curses into blessings. In them
you see the dark, sick places of our souls, and in
your mercy, understand and heal.

Janet Reeves, St John the Divine, Sandylands, Morecambe, Lancashire

Let your light shine before others, so that they may
see your good works and give glory to your Father
in heaven. *Matthew 5:16*

Heavenly Father, there are so many times among
the noise and activity of normal family life when I

75

think of your parenthood and how you too have
known the vast range of emotions each mother
or father experiences. I thank you every day,
Father, for the joy of being a parent, and in trust
and faith I bring to you the responsibilities of
guiding and caring for my growing family. Give
me your wisdom when they bring me their
problems; give me your understanding as they
struggle to become independent; give me your
love when they are being unlovable; give me your
strength when their crises threaten to swamp the
harmony of family life. Above all, Father, give me
your grace, that the teaching and example I give
to my children is to your glory and that your
peace may be at the very centre of our family.

St Paul's MU, Little Marsden, Lancashire

I kneel before the Father, from whom his whole
family in heaven and on earth derives its name.

Ephesians 3:14—15

O God, please help me to place myself and all my cares in your capable hands; help me to 'let go' and accept your love and comfort at this stressful time. I know that often, quite wrongly, I feel that you are not aware of my needs especially when things do not happen as I wish, but such is my human failing.

Lord, you in your infinite wisdom and love are far-seeing; I know that you have a purpose for everyone and I must learn from you. If only I could always remember this and trust you more.

Help me to place myself in your loving hands, to always recognize and appreciate your goodness and mercy, so that when the cares and tribulations of this world try to take me over, please let me come to you to hear you say 'Peace ... be still.'

Gladys Davies, All Saints' MU, Grendon, Warwickshire

We know that in all things God works for the good of those who love him, who have been called according to his purpose. *Romans 8:28*

Father of all, we give you thanks for the lovely,
fleeting gift of time. Make us conscious of our
responsibility for the way we use it. In our busy
years with demands of work, home, children and
absorbing interests, help us to avoid feeling guilty
if we are not filling every minute with activity. Let
us take time to be still and know that you are God.
In our times of relaxation, on holiday and enforced
idleness, during illness and the restrictions
of advancing years, help us to make good use of
the extra time available to us, to enrich our
relationships with you Lord and with other people.
We ask this in the name of Jesus, who was never
rushed or hurried but always had time for the
demands made on him and always had time for
prayer.

Kathleen Davidson, Morpeth, Northumberland

With the Lord a day is like a thousand years, and a
thousand years are like a day. *2 Peter 3:8*

Sometimes my life seems like a maze —
Which way to turn, or where to go?
There are so many different ways
We tend to lose the path we know.

It seems to me I'm circling round,
That I've been this way before,
But every time I stop to think
The doubts confront me more.

The journey is a lonely one
Travelling without a friend,
But following in Christ's footsteps
He guides us to the end.

Muriel Canzini, Thornton Dale MU, North Yorkshire

I am the way and the truth and the life. *John 14:6*

Receive my silence, Lord, when I am lost
   for words to pray.
Look deep into my heart and read the words
   I cannot say.
I long to tell my fears but dare not in case
   I fear renew;
In silence and humility I bring my cares to you.
Hear me, help me, love me, because you know
   I care,
And in my silence read a feeble but fervent
   prayer.

Millie Sherwood, Knowbury & Coreley MU, *Shropshire*

We do not know what we ought to pray for, but the
Spirit himself intercedes for us with groans that
words cannot express. *Romans 8:26*

Lord, how can I ever thank you for all you
    have done for me?
For the sheltering care and tenderness, and
    endless loyalty.
For all the paths your love has smoothed; the
    guidance from your hands,
The consolation of your Word in a world
    that misunderstands.
For the patience, Lord, you have had with
    me when I thought that I knew best,
For the sanctuary of your heart when I
    sorely needed rest,
The lamp of hope you held for me above
    dark ways and rough.
Oh how can I ever thank you Lord, or ever
    do enough?

Gladys Finnie, St Mary's MU, Ellon, Aberdeenshire

Give thanks in all circumstances, for this is God's
will for you in Christ Jesus. *1 Thessalonians 5:18*

Each day is different; thank you Lord,
As we try to listen to your word.

As the pattern changes from day to day
May we always find the time to pray.

As we rush about from place to place
Living at such a hectic pace

May we find a haven of quiet and peace
Where we can relax and pray with ease.

So once again, dear Lord, we pray
As life goes on from day to day.

Liz Curtis, Stonehouse MU, Gloucester

He who respects the day has the Lord in mind in
doing so. *Romans 14:6*

Dear Lord, yours is the Still Small Voice
That speaks within my soul;
That whispers to my heart and mind,
The prompting, gentle, firm but kind
That leads me through the narrow way
Towards your final goal.

Help me to listen, and to trust
Your guidance from above;
That I may do your will not mine,
And seek to find the Cause Divine
That gives my life its purpose
In your everlasting love.

Mary Harris, Clayton with Keymer MU, West Sussex

After the earthquake came a fire, but the Lord was
not in the fire. After the fire came a gentle whisper.

1 Kings 19:12

As I End My Day

❧ Lord, you are with me as I end my day.
   Give me your forgiveness.

Lord God, as we shall be going to bed shortly, help us to sleep and wake up well, and so to be amongst those people who will return safely to your presence tomorrow, Lord, to give you more thanks and praise.

Christina Sosanya, MU Overseas Links Correspondent, Stoke Newington, London

When you are in your beds, search your hearts and be silent. *Psalm 4:4*

Lord God, creator of the world, we praise you, we bless you, we glorify you. We ask your forgiveness for all the things we have done wrong; we are truly sorry; help us to forgive those who have hurt us.

Margaret Froggatt, St Oswald's MU, Flamborough, North Yorkshire

Forgive, and you will be forgiven. *Luke 6:37*

87

Please God, give me strength and courage to say
the right things, to do the right things, never to be
afraid or do anything silly, and thank you for today.

Olive Jackson, St Paul's Church, Blackley, Manchester

I eagerly expect and hope that I will in no way be
ashamed, but will have sufficient courage so that
now as always Christ will be exalted in my body,
whether by life or by death. *Philippians 1:20*

Lord Jesus, help me to find you when my faith is
weak. Let me know you are walking by my side.
Give me ears to hear your knock on the door so
that I may open it.

Alma Cole, Stockton, Cleveland

The apostles said to the Lord, 'Increase our faith.'

Luke 17:5

Grant us, O Lord, so to live that we are not afraid to die; so to die that we rejoice to live again.

K. Milne, Banbury, Sheffield

God so loved the world that he gave his one and only Son, that whoever believes in him shall not perish but have eternal life. *John 3:16*

Dear God and Father, please help me to bear the loneliness and sadness of parting. 'Love endureth for ever' – help me to remember that always.

Barbara Riddett, MU, Norwich diocese

And now these three remain: faith, hope and love. But the greatest of these is love. *1 Corinthians 13:13*

Dear Lord, now I am on my own you seem to
be with me more; I am sure my loved one is with
you. I think of all the things you have helped me
with and pray you will continue. Thank you for
your love.

Lilian Jasper, St Stephen's MU, Norbury, London

For I am convinced that neither death nor life ...
nor anything else in all creation, will be able to
separate us from the love of God that is in Christ
Jesus our Lord. *Romans 8:38–39*

❧

Dear Father God, please remember all elderly
people; at home, in hospital or in nursing homes.
Be with them in their loneliness and anxiety, help
them to overcome their difficulties; guide friends
and relatives to be tolerant, patient, understanding,
caring and above all loving.

Mary Parsons, St Mary's MU, Brecon, Powys

Jesus said to his mother 'Dear woman, here is your son', and to the disciple, 'Here is your mother'. From that time on, this disciple took her into his home. *John 19:26—27*

Dear Lord, take away the strain and stress of this day and replace our tensions with your loving peace and presence. Help us to forget who we are, and think only who you are. Let us rest in your love and feel the strength of the power of prayer in this quiet time when we in our helplessness listen to you for guidance in our daily lives.

Jennifer Hayward, Bretton MU, Peterborough diocese

He who turns dawn to darkness, and treads the high places of the earth — the Lord God Almighty is his name. *Amos 4:13*

God our Father, we pray for all who have reached
the age of retirement. Lord, we know that we are
all of value to you, whatever our age. Bless those
who are having to adapt to a slower pace of life.
Help them to rejoice in shared memories of joy and
laughter, sadness and disappointment. May they
praise you for the past and trust you for the future.

Maureen Sutton, St Michael's MU, Macclesfield, Cheshire

Is not wisdom found among the aged? Does not long
life bring understanding? *Job 12:12*

ᘓ

Lord, when I am afraid, please give me strength.
When I am troubled, comfort me. If I am angry,
calm my thoughts and when I feel ashamed, remind
me of your forgiveness. When I am glad, let me
remember your unfailing goodness to me. When my
footsteps falter, walk beside me. When I forget you,

as I often do, then Lord, forgive me, but do not forget me.

Norma Lethbridge, Hanwood MU, Shrewsbury, Shropshire

Turn to me and have mercy on me, as you always do to those who love your name. Direct my footsteps according to your word. *Psalm 119:132–133*

I remember the prayer I used to say as I knelt by my bed as a child: 'Lord Jesus, send the angels to watch over me' at the end of each day. As I grew older I came to believe that angels don't just live in heaven up above; the folks we meet every day where we live are human angels, those known for their understanding, their care and their love. Thank you for them, Lord.

Pat Cobban, St Luke's MU, Haverigg, Cumbria

Do not forget to entertain strangers, for by so doing some people have entertained angels without knowing it. *Hebrews 13:2*

Lord, I did not praise you nor thank you for all you have given me. Instead I lived on the sensations of the day, which caused me to dare to act without you, leading me to places of arridity until I needed to drink, and then I knew how far I had travelled away from you. Your grace is instant; it is overflowing and it flowed with my tears. It brought me back to life and I praise you for it.

Lindsay Nevin, St Lawrence & St Swithin, Winchester

As the deer pants for streams of water, so my soul pants for you, O God. *Psalm 42:1*

Heavenly Father, open our hearts to see the grudges that we bear against real and imagined hurts. Help us to be ready to listen when others ask our pardon. Help us to forgive those who do not ask for forgiveness; as you are ready to forgive us when we do wrong, even when we hurt you deeply. We ask this in Jesus' name, who died that all could be forgiven.

Ricky Chilvers, Market Deeping MU, Peterborough

Then Peter came to Jesus and asked, 'Lord, how many times shall I forgive my brother when he sins against me? Up to seven times?' Jesus answered, 'I tell you, not seven times, but seventy-seven times.'

Matthew 18:21–22

Please Lord, give us understanding when a loved one has been taken away, not when life's span was over but by violence on an ordinary day. May the families of all those affected be comforted in their loss and when they wake up each morning still fix their eyes firmly on the Cross.

The Mothers' Union, Peterborough diocese

'Where have you laid him?' he asked. 'Come and see, Lord,' they replied. Jesus wept. *John 11:34–35*

Almighty God, our Father in heaven, who is the source of comfort and strength, uplift our dying friend and her family. Give them all strength and faith to accept your way in the days to come. Grant that she may find an inner peace and understanding knowing that you are always with her.

The Mothers' Union, Province of Ireland

Jesus said to her, 'I am the resurrection and the life. He who believes in me will live, even though he dies; and whoever lives and believes in me will never die.'

John 11:25–26

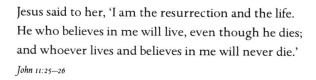

Lord Jesus Christ, you went through the agony of facing your own death, and cried out to God that if it were possible it might not happen – yet you were given strength to go to the Cross. I come to you with all my confusion and pain, my hopes and my fears. I find it hard to accept that all this is really happening. I have many doubts and questions. I sometimes feel angry with you, yet I need your help and strength. I pour out to you my grief, my tears, my regrets and my guilt. Please bear with me and give me your peace.

Irene Lomax, St James' Church, Broughton, Greater Manchester

Jesus said, 'Abba, Father ... everything is possible for you. Take this cup from me. Yet not what I will, but what you will.' *Mark 14:36*

Almighty God, from the age of two you have been my only Father. You led me, nurtured me and guided me. When I was a teenager, confused, lost, lonely and lacking in confidence, you found me and reassured me. When my mother breathed her last and left me, you gave me strength and comforted me. Thank you for being there when I needed a Father, Mother, friend and comforter, and for sending your Son Jesus Christ to be with me today, tomorrow and always.

Rosémia Brown, St John's MU, Hackney, London

Jesus Christ is the same yesterday and today and forever. *Hebrews 13:8*

Father, the evening comes and it is time to sleep. As you have been with me through the day, so be with me through the coming night. In your mercy forgive the wrong that I have done. Bless my loved ones and strengthen those who need my prayers tonight. Keep me in your grace and peace. When I sleep, watch over me in your goodness, and when I lie awake fill my heart with thoughts of you. Give me, dear Lord, rest and refreshment, that when morning comes I may greet the day with confidence and hope.

Joan Stannard, Carlisle Cathedral, Cumbria

I will lie down and sleep in peace, for you alone,
O Lord, make me dwell in safety. *Psalm 4:8*

Faithful Father, never changing, with us
through all the passing years, may we walk in
your love all our days and reflect your glory in
our lives.

For this wonderful earth and all creation —
    great God, we praise you.
For all that is noble and good in humankind —
    great God, we thank you.
For sending Jesus Christ to redeem us from our
    sins — Lord God, we love you.
For being our heavenly Father and offering us
    eternal life — almighty God, we worship you.

*Marion Holmes, St Michael & St Helen's, Quarry Hill,
Almondbury, West Yorkshire*

Praise the Lord, all his works everywhere in his
dominion. Praise the Lord, O my soul. *Psalm 103:22*

Dear Father,
Thank you for this bed of mine and bless all who
    are sleeping rough.
Thank you for this warm bedding and bless all
    who are cold and frightened.

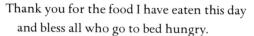

Thank you for the food I have eaten this day
and bless all who go to bed hungry.
Thank you for the roof over my head and bless
all who are homeless.
Thank you for the safety of my children and
bless all whose children are missing.
Thank you for the peace of the neighbourhood
and bless and comfort all who fear the knock
at the door.
Thank you, Father, for everything you have
given me and make me mindful of the needs of
others, for Jesus' sake.

Athalie Lytle, Portsmouth Cathedral MU, Hampshire

The Lord bless you and keep you; the Lord make
his face shine upon you and be gracious to you; the
Lord turn his face towards you and give you peace.

Numbers 6:24–26

He takes away our sorrow, he tends the
    wounded heart
He comforts us in sadness when we from
    friends must part.
He gives us strength to persevere when we
    are feeling low,
He gently pulls us from the brink, he
    lets his mercy flow.
He takes away our weakness, he fills our
    hearts with peace,
His Holy Spirit strengthens us, he bids our
    worries cease.

Marion Carrington, St Helen's MU, Hemsworth, West Yorkshire

Even though I walk through the valley of the
shadow of death, I will fear no evil, for you are with
me. *Psalm 23:4*

I pray, dear Lord, that you will be
Always very close to me.
Place my footsteps in your own
So I won't stray in paths unknown.
Hold my hands in yours that heal
The lonely and heartbroken.
May I know I'm in your care
Although no word is spoken.

*Marion Lacy, St Paul's MU, Wood Green, Wednesbury,
West Midlands*

The Lord will watch over your coming and going
both now and for evermore. *Psalm 121:8*

God, be my resting place and my protection
In hours of trouble, defeat and dejection.
May I never give way to self-pity and sorrow,
May I always be sure of a better tomorrow.
May I stand undaunted come what may,

Secure in the knowledge I have only to pray
And ask my Creator and Father above
To keep me serene in his grace and his love.

Kitty Stredder, St Mary's MU, Hitchin, Hertfordshire

Ask and it will be given to you; seek and you will
find; knock and the door will be opened to you.

Matthew 7:7

Lord, my heart grieves for you.
You gave your life for me –
I know that sorrow and bitter death
Have caused you suffering for my sake
Because you loved me –
You loved me to the end.

Crowned with thorns that I might live,
Wounded for my transgressions –
Rejected that I might stand

Accepted on your right hand
For life everlasting.
You loved me with a love so vast,
For you loved me to the bitter end.

Marjorie White, St Philip & All Saints' MU, Kew, Surrey

But God demonstrates his own love for us in this:
While we were still sinners, Christ died for us.

Romans 5:8

Index of First Lines